ST. PAUL'S CATHEDRAL

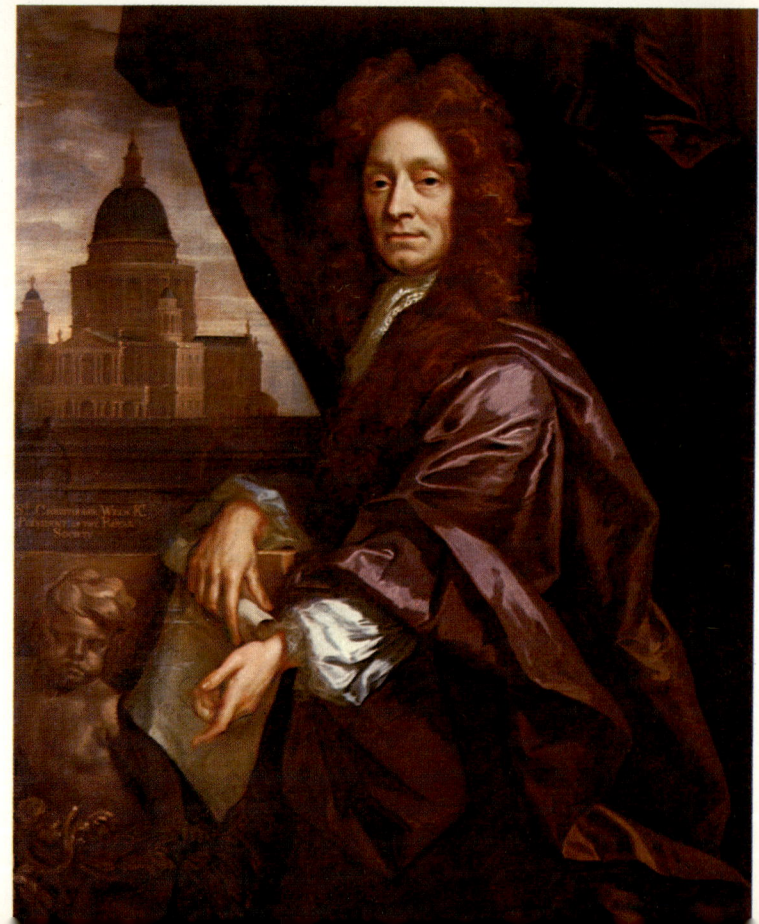

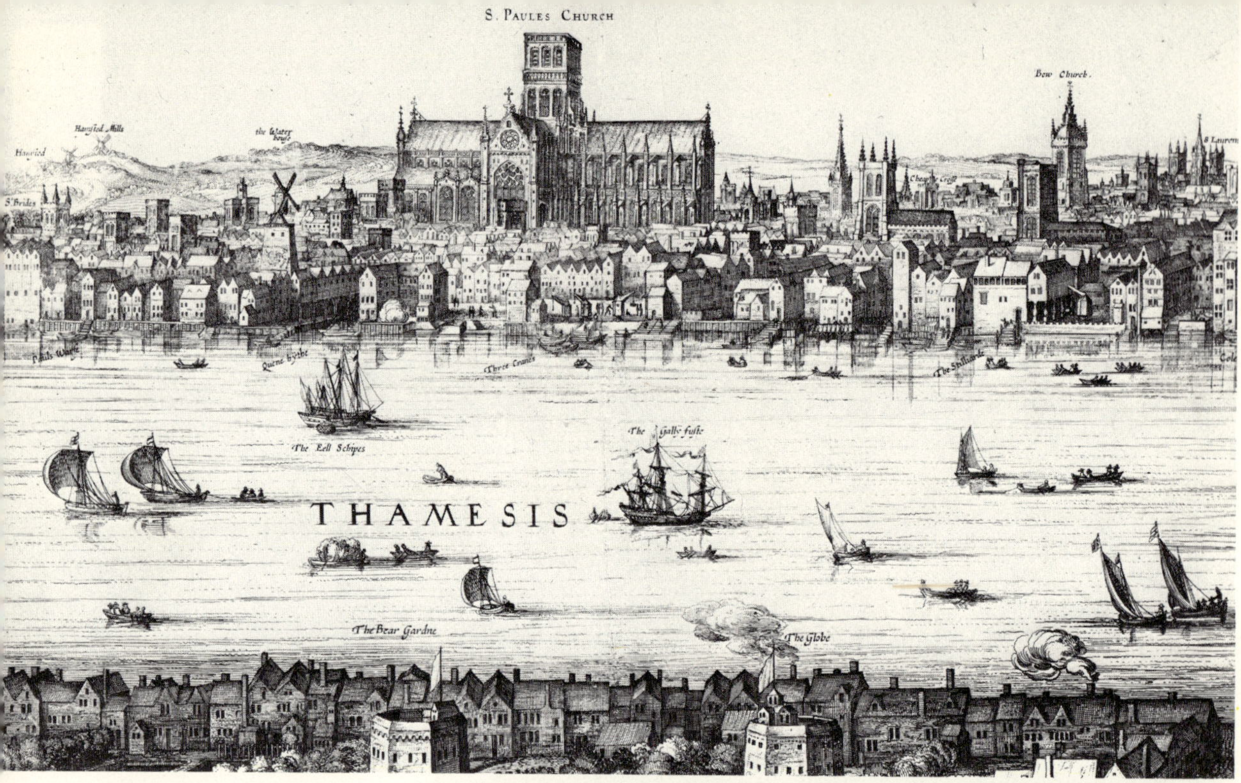
S. Paules Church
Bow Church
THAMESIS
The Bear Gardne
The Globe

ABOVE: *This engraving, made by Vischer in the early 17th century, shows part of the City of London with the great Gothic Cathedral, known as Old St. Paul's, dominating the skyline. Old St. Paul's was reduced to a ruin in the great fire of 1666.*

RIGHT: *The architect of St. Paul's, Sir Christopher Wren. He was in his early sixties when this portrait was painted by John Closterman in about 1695. It is in the possession of the Royal Society, of which Wren was president, and a reminder that he was also eminent in the sphere of experimental science, to which his early career was directed. Born in 1632, at East Knoyle, Wiltshire, he was appointed Savilian Professor of Astronomy at Oxford in 1661, but soon afterwards turned his attention to architecture. He was a member of the commission set up in 1663 to consider the restoration of "Old St. Paul's". In September, 1666, the year the cathedral perished in the Fire of London, Wren was asked to design its successor. He produced three designs for the cathedral. The plan finally accepted was the "Warrant Design", but in building the cathedral Wren made his own variations.*

OVERLEAF: *The Chapel of St. Dunstan is often used for the daily celebrations of Holy Communion and is also available for private prayer. The hangings behind the altar were the gift of the Friends of St. Paul's.*

ST. PAUL'S CATHEDRAL

Sir David Floyd Ewin, MVO, OBE, MA

FOR thirteen and a half centuries a cathedral dedicated to the honour of Saint Paul has stood upon the summit of Ludgate Hill. Sir Christopher Wren's great Renaissance church which rises majestically over the City is the fifth to bear the name of London's patron saint.

The history of St. Paul's begins with the consecration of Mellitus as bishop of the East Saxons by St. Augustine of Canterbury in 604 A.D. His cathedral, which was probably a

★

ABOVE: *On the terrifying night of 29th December 1940 a large part of the City of London perished in a fire-bomb raid. St. Paul's, as though by a miracle, escaped severe damage.*

wooden structure, was founded by Ethelbert, King of Kent, who endowed it with the Manor of Tillingham in Essex—an estate which, to this day, is still held by the Dean and Chapter.

The first cathedral was destroyed by fire—a peril which through the centuries has beset all five churches. It was rebuilt in stone in 675–685 by the saintly Bishop Erkenwald whose shrine attracted many pilgrims to the cathedral throughout the middle ages. This church was destroyed by the Vikings in the ninth century and again rebuilt in 962.

In 1087 the Saxon church was also burned down. Rebuilding, which began almost at once, had the support of William Rufus, son of William the Conqueror, whom he had just suc-

ceeded as king. Maurice, a Norman, and sometime chaplain and chancellor to William the Conqueror, had been appointed Bishop of London the previous year. He seized the opportunity to build a cathedral on a vaster scale than anything previously envisaged in London. This cathedral, familiarly known as "Old St. Paul's", was destroyed in the Great Fire of London in 1666.

"Old St. Paul's" stood within spacious precincts enclosed by walls. The line of these walls was marked by the course of Creed Lane and Ave Maria Lane on the west, Paternoster Row on the north, Old Change on the east, and Carter Lane on the south. In the walls of the precincts were six gates—the principal one being on Ludgate Hill; the second at Paul's

Alley, leading to "Little North Dore"; the third at Canon's Alley, leading to the north transept door; the fourth, called Little Gate, leading from Cheapside to Paul's Cross; the fifth, St. Augustine's Gate, at the end of Watling Street; the sixth leading up from the river to the south transept.

As at first designed, the cathedral consisted of a nave of twelve bays, transepts and a short apsidal choir, all built in the round-arched, or Norman, style. Work on the choir was delayed by a fire in 1136 and it was not in use until 1148 when the remains of St. Erkenwald were translated to a new shrine behind the high altar. The upper stages of the nave and the west end were completed by the end of the twelfth century. About 1220 the great spire was begun and improvements were made to the choir. The cathedral was finished and dedicated in 1240.

Immediately eastwards of the cathedral the parishioners of St. Faith had built their parish church. As services in the cathedral became more elaborate, it was decided to pull down the Norman choir and to replace it with a larger one in the more graceful Gothic style. Work began about 1258 and was completed by 1314. This new choir was carried twelve bays eastward and involved the destruction of the church of St. Faith. In compensation the parishioners were granted use of part of the crypt beneath the new choir as their parish church, a privilege they enjoyed until Old St. Paul's was eventually destroyed.

The length of the building grew to 596 feet. Not only was St. Paul's the largest church in England but it was surpassed in size among European cathedrals only by Seville and Milan.

The spire, 489 feet high and the loftiest that had ever been built, was completed in 1315. It was struck by lightning in 1447 and was not repaired until 1462 when the weathercock upon a ball capable of holding ten bushels of corn was re-erected.

Surrounding the Norman cathedral were the bishop's palace, the deanery, and the houses of the residentiary canons. In 1332 a chapter house was built against the south side of the cathedral by William of Ramsey, one of the foremost architects of the day. Remains of the cloisters of the chapter house, and the foundations of two buttresses of the chapter house itself, can still be seen in the gardens on the south side of the nave.

The most famous part of the precincts in the middle ages was Paul's Cross, an open air pulpit and the scene of many fiery sermons, particularly during the Reformation. To the east lay the Cathedral School which was refounded in 1512 by Dean Colet. This school—now very well known as St. Paul's School—was transferred to Hammersmith in 1884.

Continued on page 6

*

LEFT: *All Souls' Chapel contains the Kitchener Memorial commemorating the spirit of sacrifice shown by the Army in the 1914–18 war. The figure of the Field Marshal in white marble is by Sir William Reid Dick, R.A.*

RIGHT: *This memorial to Arthur Wellesley, first Duke of Wellington (1769–1852), is in the north aisle. Started in 1857 the monument took twenty years to complete.*

In 1377, Bishop Courtenay of London summoned John Wyclif, the great writer and reformer, before a convocation at St. Paul's on a charge of heresy. John of Gaunt, son of Edward III and at that time the virtual ruler of England, appeared in support of Wyclif. A riotous mob, hostile to John of Gaunt, surged into the Lady Chapel where the trial was in progress and created such a disturbance that the proceedings were abandoned.

The 14th century brought great and splendid changes to the interior of the cathedral. The floors were paved with marble and the relics of St. Erkenwald, which had achieved a reputation for working miracles, were translated to another and more magnificent shrine adorned with gold. Sumptuous chantry chapels were built where Masses were offered for the souls of the founders. In 1400 the body of the deposed Richard II was brought to St. Paul's to lie in state for three days.

During the early 15th century, St. Paul's was the setting for many trials for heresy and witchcraft. The unhappy souls found guilty passed from its precincts to nearby Smithfield to die by burning at the stake.

A state occasion of great magnificence at the beginning of the 16th century was the marriage of Arthur, Prince of Wales, to Princess Catherine of Aragon, but within six months Catherine was a widow. Seven years later, quietly at Greenwich, she married her brother-in-law, Henry VIII. Henry frequently attended St. Paul's on state occasions—one of them being the proclamation of Queen Catherine's nephew as the Emperor Charles V. Cardinal Wolsey, almost as resplendent a figure as the king himself, was often present in the cathedral.

The reigns of Henry VIII and Edward VI saw great changes in the church of England; at the onset of the Reformation the churches were despoiled of their wealth and treasures and the services reduced to great

Continued on page 8

★

LEFT: *This view of the north aisle shows the memorial to Frederick, Lord Leighton (1830–96), and that of General Charles George Gordon, killed at Khartoum in 1885.*

RIGHT: *The nave looking east: a noble vista of arcades, clerestory and saucer domes.*

simplicity. St. Paul's suffered no less than others in this respect, being deprived not only of her treasures but of much of her revenue as well. This lack of money was a contributory factor in the cathedral's later structural decay. On St. Barnabas's Day, 1549, the high altar was pulled down and in its place a plain table, for the administration of the sacrament, was set up in the middle of the choir. The reredos was hacked to ruins and, among the tombs, only that of John of Gaunt was by royal command spared damage.

Although the old ritual and some of the former glory was restored during the five-year reign of Mary I, it was again suppressed on the accession of her half-sister, Elizabeth I. The Latin services were discontinued and the images which had been restored by Mary quietly removed at night.

The new Protestant dean, Alexander Nowell, who died in 1602 at the great age of 91, frequently preached before Elizabeth. In the course of his sermon on Ash Wednesday, 1565, the dean attacked the use of images but was interrupted by the autocratic Elizabeth who bade him "To your text, Mr. Dean, we have heard enough".

After the Reformation, houses and shops were erected right up to the very walls of the cathedral. The old practice of using the long nave, popularly known as "Paul's Walk", as a passage-way, and of conducting business there, grew to scandalous lengths. Against a background of babble and chatter, with tradespeople selling their wares and horses being led through the building, services were held in the choir. In 1598 Bishop Bancroft was informed that it was used as "a common passage and thoroughfare for all kinds of Burden bearing people as Colliers with sacks of coal . . . also a daily receptacle for rogues and beggars however diseased, to the great offence of religious-minded people". Despite protests, this state of affairs continued until the end of the Norman cathedral. It was even revived in 1724 in the new cathedral but was finally abolished by order of Bishop Gibson.

Shortly after Elizabeth became queen there occurred the first calamity that led to the decay of Old St. Paul's. On the afternoon of 4th June 1561, during a severe thunderstorm, the spire was again struck by lightning. In an age when lightning

Continued on page 10

LEFT, top: *One of the fine mosaics in the eastern part of the cathedral. This is in one of the saucer domes and illustrates scenes from the Book of Genesis.*
LEFT: *The font in the north transept which was made by Francis Bird and* was finished in 1727. ABOVE: *The Dome Area. Here nave, transept and chancel aisles meet at the domed crossing. The pulpit, first used in 1964, was designed by John Seely, 2nd Lord Mottistone. The wrought-iron gates seen at the en-* trance to the north choir aisle were made by a Frenchman, *Jean Tijou. The sanctuary screens and the balustrading of the Geometrical Staircase, shown on pages 11 and 24 of this book, were also made by Jean Tijou.*

conductors were unknown, the spire soon caught alight and burnt downwards to the square tower and so to the roofs which were badly damaged before the fire was finally extinguished. Repairs commenced with commendable speed; an improvised roof was constructed of boards and lead, though it was not until the following November that services could again be held in the choir. But enthusiasm soon waned; three years later there was no permanent roof over the transepts which Bishop Grindal then re-roofed at his own expense at a cost of £720. Although no attempt was made to re-erect the spire, the cathedral was usable and, on Sunday, 27th November 1588, Elizabeth I came to the great service of thanksgiving for victory over the Spanish armada. She was carried to the cathedral amid a blare of trumpets in a chariot "like a throne" drawn by four white horses. The lower battlements of the cathedral were bedecked with ensigns captured from the enemy's ships.

The fire, and the consequent inadequate protection against the wea-

ther for so long, caused the structure to deteriorate still further. James I took a personal interest in a project of restoration and in 1620 a Royal Commission was set up. A survey was carried out and plans drawn up for repairs to the extent of over £22,000 but work did not commence until 1628 when the vigorous William Laud became bishop and Inigo Jones, the famous architect, was appointed King's Surveyor.

Jones demolished the houses and shops that had been built up against the cathedral and encased the nave in ashlar masonry with windows in the classical style in place of the medieval tracery. He altered the west front by removing the original triple Norman entrances and erected a splendid though incongruous portico in the Corinthian order surmounted by a balustrade, and attempted to strengthen and patch-up the entire fabric. This work, costing approximately £100,000, took place between 1634 and 1643 when the Civil War put a stop to building.

The Parliamentarians then appro-

priated the £17,000 remaining in the repair fund and, to pay their troops, sold the scaffolding—as a result of which part of the south transept collapsed. The clergy lost their benefices, their incomes were confiscated, the few remaining cathedral treasures were dispersed, and Cornelius Burgess, a puritan preacher, was installed at a stipend of £400 a year. The east end of the cathedral was used by him as a preaching house; the nave became a cavalry barracks for the puritan soldiery; the windows were all smashed, and the carved woodwork burnt as firewood.

Continued on page 14

*

ABOVE: *The Chapel of Modern Martyrs commemorates anglican martyrs since 1850. All the known names are recorded in a marble casket. The altar was formerly in the Jesus Chapel (now the American Memorial Chapel).*

RIGHT: *One of the greater glories of the cathedral: the sanctuary screens by Jean Tijou. Tijou worked in St. Paul's Cathedral between 1691 and 1709.*

ABOVE: *The American Memorial Chapel is the tribute of the people of Britain to the 28,000 American citizens who, from their base in the United Kingdom, met their death in the Second World War. The chapel was dedicated on 26th November 1958.*

RIGHT: *This view shows the high altar and also the American Memorial Chapel at the back. The altar is of Sicilian marble. Surmounting the dome of the baldacchino is the figure of Our Lord in Triumph, with four gold angels around Him. The choir stalls are by Grinling Gibbons.*

The tombs erected since the Reformation—among them those of Sir Philip Sidney and his sister, the Countess of Pembroke, one of the few learned women of her age—were badly mutilated. Thus the ravages of the Civil War completed the deterioration which had commenced with the fire of 1561 and by 1660, when Charles II was restored to the throne, St. Paul's was in the final stages of decay and despoliation—"a loathsome Golgotha" as one contemporary described it.

In 1663 another Royal Commission on St. Paul's was set up. The exact date when Sir Christopher Wren was consulted is not known, but his report was issued on 1st May 1666. It caused some heat when discussed by the commissioners but eventually they agreed, in Evelyn's words, to Wren's proposal for "a noble cupola, a form of church-building not as yet known in England, but of wonderful grace". It is pointless to speculate on the incongruous appearance thus planned for St. Paul's, with Inigo Jones' classical nave and Wren's classical cupola joined to the Gothic choir, for the cathedral was totally destroyed in the Great Fire of London in 1666.

It was hoped that the cathedral would escape and merchants stored their goods in the churchyard and in the church of St. Faith in the crypt. But the ferocity of the fire leaped across the precincts from the burning houses nearby, setting light to scaffolding around the tower. Soon the entire building was ablaze and nothing remained unharmed but parts of the walls and some columns. The only monument to survive was the effigy of Dr. John Donne who was dean from 1621 to his death in 1631. This can be seen today in the south choir aisle.

At first, it was thought that the ruins could be restored and the west end of the cathedral, which was the least damaged part, was patched up for services in 1667. Work began the following year in clearing the rubble from the rest of the building, and shoring up the walls, but the futility of the scheme was soon demonstrated by the collapse of a column, thus endangering the surrounding structure.

A complete rebuilding was now obviously essential and on 2nd July 1668, Dean Sancroft wrote to Wren on behalf of the commissioners, desiring him to prepare a design for submission to the king. Thus began the plans for the fifth and present cathedral but seven years were to pass before the first stone was laid. Wren, now Surveyor-General, produced three designs.

The first, the so-called "New Model" design, was completed in 1670, and received the king's approval but was rejected by the com-

Continued on page 16

★

LEFT: *When the Fire of London destroyed Old St. Paul's this spectral effigy of Dr. John Donne was saved. Donne became Dean of St. Paul's in 1621 and died in 1631, having previously posed in his shroud for a painting from which this white marble statue was made.*

RIGHT: *St. Paul's had no Lady Chapel until after World War Two, when this one was constructed and Wren's original high altar re-erected in it. Part of his organ screen (removed in 1858) frames the statue of the Blessed Virgin.*

missioners who found that it was untraditional in that there were no aisles to the choir and no proper nave.

By September 1673 Wren had completed a much bolder design, known as the "Great Model", and built a model which may still be seen in the cathedral trophy room. Made in oak and measuring 20 feet in length, this superb and unique structure cost £600 and took nine months to make. Wren thus ensured that the commissioners should be under no misapprehension as to the appearance of his proposed classical masterpiece. This was conceived on the plan of a Greek cross with a vast dome over the central area and with a smaller domed vestibule and portico to the west. Again the king approved the design and again the commissioners

rejected it on the same ground that it was not traditional.

Wren's third and last plan is known as the "Warrant Design". More traditional, it was based on the Latin cross plan, the western arm (the nave) being longer than the eastern (the choir), with a domed crossing between nave and choir. There were shallow transepts on the north and south, and a western portico. This design was accepted by the king, though acceptance was not unanimous among the commissioners. The king, a shrewd reader of men, probably understood something of the cross-currents between the architect and the commissioners and the royal warrant authorising the design in April 1675 permitted "variations, rather ornamental than essential". From this

warrant the design takes its name. The Latin cross plan was evidently essential, but freedom was permissible in its actual interpretation.

Wren was not slow to make an alteration in plan. The main change was the substitution of three bays for five in the nave, thus equalising nave and choir with the dome placed cen-

*

ABOVE: *The O.B.E. Chapel at the east end of the crypt is the shrine of the Order of the British Empire, instituted by King George V in 1917. It was designed by Lord Mottistone, Surveyor of the Fabric of St. Paul's Cathedral 1957–63. The chapel is enclosed by wrought-iron screens inset with paintings in grisaille of the founder and sovereigns of the order.*

trally between them. He also created a larger vestibule at the west end of the building.

When the site was cleared and the measurements taken, Wren asked a labourer to bring him a stone so that he might mark the centre of the new cathedral. The man brought a portion of a grave-stone from the old cathedral, inscribed with the word "*Resurgam*" —"I shall rise again". This so impressed Wren that he had this word incised on the exterior of the new cathedral and it may be seen beneath the carved representation of a phoenix rising from flames in the pediment above the great south door.

The foundation stone was laid, probably with some Masonic ceremony, on 21st June 1675. As Surveyor-General, Wren was responsible for many other projects. He delegated the constructional work to a splendid team, attending himself to super-intend once a week, usually on Saturdays. Progress, however, was slow. After Charles II's death in 1685, a new set of men attained to public life, some of whom were out of sympathy with the architect's methods. In 1697, when the choir was open for Divine Service, a faction of the House of Commons were so dissatisfied with the rate of progress that it was proposed that half of Wren's salary should be withheld until the building was complete. This monstrous proposal met with agreement and it was not until 1711, after personally petitioning Queen Anne, that Wren received his arrears of salary.

By 1698 the main part of the cathedral was completed except for the dome and the west front. The last stone at the apex of the lantern above the cupola was placed in position by Sir Christopher's son in 1708, forty-two years after the Great Fire of 1666. Thus, the whole great enterprise of building the new St. Paul's was completed during the episcopacy of one bishop of London, one master mason in charge, and Wren—the architect and builder—had the supreme satisfaction of seeing his masterpiece completed during his lifetime.

*

RIGHT: *Sir Christopher Wren died in 1723, aged 91. Above the marble slab of his tomb is a tablet bearing the words* SI MONUMENTUM REQUIRIS CIRCUMSPICE—"*If you seek his monument, look around*".

Wren was dismissed from the Surveyor-Generalship in 1718; he was then aged 86 and his architecture already seemed old-fashioned to a new generation familiar with the baroque of Vanbrugh and Hawksmoor. He made frequent visits to his great cathedral and after one such visit on a chilly day in February 1723, he died quietly in his chair at his fireside at Hampton Court at the great age of 91. He was buried in the crypt of St. Paul's.

The enormous bulk of the cathedral as viewed from the outside is reduced to a greater unity of conception to the visitor who enters beneath the western portico. Internally, as externally, the cathedral is dominated by the enormous dome, whose height and size lend the building an airy spaciousness, flooding with light the large central space beneath. The exterior of the dome is of lead covering a timber framing. The stone lantern is supported by an unseen brick cone, and below this is the inner dome. Thus, Wren—with

his unrivalled sense of proportion—judged the proper heights for his external and internal domes, and his engineering genius enabled him to carry it out. The Cross surmounting the dome and lantern stands 365 feet above the pavement, well over 100 feet lower than the cross on the spire of the Old St. Paul's.

The western façade is in the Renaissance style. A portico of twelve columns in pairs stands at the head of a noble flight of steps. Placed between the two towers is another portico of eight columns in pairs and crowning this is a high pediment containing in the tympanum a spirited sculptured group representing the Conversion of Saint Paul, by Francis Bird, while on the apex a colossal statue of London's patron saint dominates all.

Wren was a genius in choosing the ablest artists and craftsmen of his day, and it is inside the cathedral that their work can be best appreciated. Pride of place falls to Grinling Gibbons who carved the choir stalls during the 1690's—one of the finest examples of carved woodwork in existence today. The superb oak organ cases and choir stalls were made under the direction of Charles Hopson, the joiner. Another great craftsman, Jean Tijou, was responsible for the magnificent ironwork sanctuary gates in the north and south choir aisles and the spiral Dean's Staircase in the south-western tower.

From Wren's day until the 19th-century alterations, a screen bearing the organ enclosed the choir at the western end. The organ had been used by Handel and the organ cases were carved by Grinling Gibbons. The screen was removed to open an uninterrupted vista from west to east of the cathedral, a view not originally intended, and the organ case was divided into two parts. At the same time, a great marble reredos was erected behind the high altar.

The crypt, said to be the largest in Europe, is approached by steps from the south transept. To the right as one enters lies the simple grave of Sir Christopher Wren, one of the first to be interred in the cathedral. In the floor nearby rest the remains of some of England's greatest artists, among them Millais, Holman Hunt, Reynolds and Turner. Also famed in their time were those buried in Old St. Paul's whose names are listed in the Chapel of St. Christopher. Another chapel, that of the Most Excellent Order of the British Empire at the east end, is one of two in St. Paul's dedicated to Orders of Chivalry.

The Duke of Wellington's body lies in an immense 17-ton tomb; his remains were carried on the funeral car made from the metal of captured guns which can be seen at the extreme west end of the crypt. Also accorded a state funeral was Lord Nelson, now enshrined directly beneath the centre of the dome, with his fellow admirals, Collingwood and Lord Northesk, lying to the south and north of him. A memorial to Florence Nightingale is nearby, and many naval and military commanders are buried or commemorated in the crypt, their monuments contrasting strangely with the scarred memorials salvaged from the ruins of the old cathedral. The composer Sullivan and Lawrence of Arabia are

Continued on page 21

*

LEFT: *Among the many persons buried in the crypt, only Lord Nelson and the Duke of Wellington are interred in their tombs, all other remains being below ground. The duke's sarcophagus is of Cornish porphyry on a foundation of granite.*

RIGHT: *Nelson's marble sarcophagus was part of a tomb begun in 1524 for Cardinal Wolsey. It was confiscated by Henry VIII and then lay forgotten at Windsor Castle until Nelson's death on 21st October 1805.*

ABOVE: *The inner dome, painted with the Thornhill frescoes, has a circular opening at the top through which may be seen the brick cone which carries the weight of the stone lantern. Below the windows is the Whispering Gallery.*

RIGHT, top: *The Whispering Gallery, a part of which is seen here, is remarkable for its acoustics. Anyone standing at the entrance to the gallery can hear clearly what is said on the opposite side, 107 feet away.*

RIGHT: *One of the eight frescoes in the dome illustrating the life of St. Paul. They were painted in 1716–19 by Sir James Thornhill, who was knighted and made serjeant painter to the Crown in 1720.*

two more of the many famous names recorded here.

The western towers of the cathedral are both bell-towers, the southern containing in its lower stage the geometrical staircase leading to the library and above that the clock, with an hour bell called Great Tom; beneath this hangs Great Paul, weighing nearly 17 tons, which is rung daily at 1 p.m. The northern tower contains the peal of 12 bells.

The present century has been one of anxiety for the cathedral's safety. Ominous cracks began to appear in the structure and essential repairs were carried out, particularly the strengthening of the piers which bear the 68,000 tons of dome. During the Second World War the cathedral suffered two direct hits from high-explosive bombs. One penetrated the choir roof and completely destroyed the high altar and damaged the Victorian marble reredos; the other burst between the roof and the floor of the north transept, carrying with it many tons of masonry through to the crypt.

Two bombs, which mercifully failed to explode, fell in the cathedral precincts—one by the west front, the other, a land mine, was found with its parachute close to the east end of the building. Both of these were removed by a bomb disposal squad of the Royal Engineers.

St. Paul's was also attacked by incendiary bombs and it is a tribute to the cathedral's devoted band of fire-watchers, often working under extreme danger, that they were extinguished and that the damage sustained was no worse—grievous though it was.

In 1951 the then dean of St. Paul's, Dr. Matthews, in his sermon to the members of St. Paul's Watch who helped to save the cathedral from destruction in the war years, said:

"A great building such as St. Paul's owes its fame and its place in the affections of multitudes to many causes. The genius of a great architect and of the craftsmen who assisted him created the structure, a wonder of the world; historical association and the tombs of national heroes have their part; the prayers of innumerable persons through many generations have, I doubt not, left an impression on its walls and hallowed it. But you, the members of the Watch, have added something to its treasure and have become a part of its tradition. If

21

we may suppose that the thoughts and emotions of men and women who have lived and laboured in it leave some legacy which is somehow incorporated in the building, then surely the thoughts of the company who, though for the most part far from young, scaled heights, worked stirrup pumps in darkness and peril, endured sleepless nights, and loved one another, have enriched our spiritual heritage. We will not regard this monument in a spirit of vain glory or pride but in a spirit of thankfulness. 'Not unto us O Lord, but unto thy name be the Praise'. Thank God that we were able to take part in this glorious enterprise of saving St. Paul's: and thank Him that our endeavour was crowned with success".

Essential repairs were carried out after the bombing but the post-war task of restoration was one of enormous magnitude. The new high altar, which is the British people's memorial to those of the Commonwealth who lost their lives in the war, was consecrated on 7th May 1958. A baldacchino was erected over the altar in the manner intended by Wren. Behind the altar is the American Memorial Chapel and the three stained-glass east windows which are a tribute from the British people to the 28,000 American service men and women who died whilst based on British soil and whose names are inscribed in the great Roll of Honour delivered to the Dean and Chapter in 1951 by General Eisenhower, later President of the United States.

The cathedral has succeeded in preserving the bulk of its archives, covering nearly one thousand years, but only three or four books from the medieval library and a catalogue

Continued on page 24

★

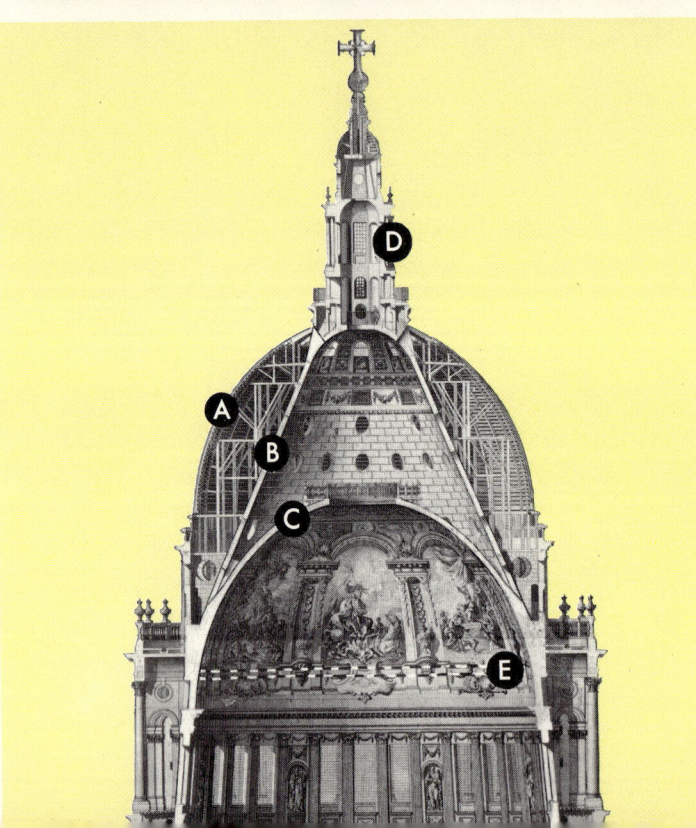

LEFT: *These two illustrations show the great dome of St. Paul's. The outer dome (marked A on the section drawing) is built of timber with a lead skin. It rests on the brick cone (B), and the stone drum. The cone takes the weight of the lantern (D) and the cross. (C) marks the inner dome, and (E) the double stainless steel chains introduced as reinforcement in 1930.*

RIGHT: *This version of W. Holman Hunt's original painting of "The Light of the World" at Keble College, Oxford, was undertaken by him in 1900 and presented to St. Paul's by the Rt. Hon. Charles Booth.*

THE
OF THE
LIGHT
WORLD

BEHOLD I STAND AT THE DOOR AND KNOCK IF ANY MAN
HEAR MY VOICE AND OPEN THE DOOR I WILL COME
IN TO HIM AND WILL SVP WITH HIM AND HE WITH ME.

of its contents remains. What survived the Reformation and the Civil War perished in the Great Fire in 1666.

The present library was constructed by Wren above the south-western chapel, and the collection of books was commenced in 1708.

St. Paul's is more than a magnificent feat of architecture and the resting place of the great and famous. First and foremost it is a place of worship. Its sole *raison d'être* is to be a place where worship is offered to God every day without intermission, with all the richness of music and ceremonial which it is possible to provide. It is here that the Bishop of London has his *cathedra* or throne, for St. Paul's is London Cathedral.

Here, on many occasions, the Sovereign comes to offer thanks for mercies received, or to mourn with them that mourn; here, many special services are held—for the knights and other ranks of the orders of St. Michael and St. George, and of the British Empire; for the Sons of the Clergy; for the Church Army; but it is the ordinary daily worship in the statutory services—Holy Communion, Mattins, and Evensong—which is the source of the strength and influence of St. Paul's. Whether or not a congregation is present is quite beside the point: worship is daily offered on behalf of the people, and if this were not so St. Paul's would no longer fulfil its duty or serve the purpose for which it was built.

*   *   *

LEFT, above: *This chapel in the south aisle became the spiritual centre of the Order of St. Michael and St. George in 1906. The order was instituted in 1818 to reward outstanding service in relation to foreign affairs.*

LEFT: *The geometrical staircase at the south-west of the cathedral was the work of William Kempster. The wrought-iron balustrading was made by Tijou. The staircase is not open for public use.*

Acknowledgments

This Official Record is published by authority of the Dean and Chapter of St. Paul's. The photographs, which are copyright, are by S. W. Newbery, Hon. F.I.I.P., F.R.P.S., with the exception of those on pages 2 and 3.